Praise for *The Medicine Woods*

"In a world altered forever by climate change, *The Medicine Woods* leads us to remember and call upon the healing properties of flora and fauna—the woodlands—because 'the earth is borrowed from our children' and the 'days of swinging grapevines . . . are slipping into oblivion.' These poems are necessary when even the memory of abundant medicinal plants and calling their names can steady, guide, and heal our souls."

—**Hilda Downer**, author of *Wiley's Last Resort*

"Danita Dodson's Zen-graced poems are restorative reminders of our indissoluble connection to creation. Keenly aware of the devastating effects of what Thoreau termed our 'war on wilderness,' Dodson evokes a spirit of oneness, her words serving as energic units of healing for an anguished planet. To this end, she summons her considerable talents as mystic, alchemist, and augur extraordinaire. Reading *The Medicine Woods* is transformative and affirming."

—**Edward Francisco**, author of *The Ever Changing Sky: Meditations on the Psalms*

"Stop and listen. You can hear it, feel it. Look more closely than you ever have. From holy trees and river stones to the five-lined skink, come and explore the healing power of the medicine woods. Deeply rooted in her Appalachian home, yet a wanderer in the wider world, Dodson is devoted to nature and spirituality. In these powerful poems, each one a meditation, she has reaffirmed for me the importance of defending the earth."

—**Ann Shurgin**, author of *While the Whippoorwill Called*

"Danita Dodson's latest book of poems, *The Medicine Woods*, is a beacon that lights the way for humankind to find healing and sanctuary in nature. Medicine lives in the woods. And nature is a meditative prayer. *The Medicine Woods* imparts that all beings on Earth are intrinsically connected. These poems implore us to consider our human footprint and take better care of our wise, ancient soils, 'to return to the wholesome ancestral voices of the keepers.'"

—**Delonda Anderson**, editor of *Appalachia Bare*

The Medicine Woods

The Medicine Woods

—————— *Poems* ——————

Danita Dodson

RESOURCE *Publications* · Eugene, Oregon

THE MEDICINE WOODS
Poems

Resource Publications
An Imprint of Wipf and Stock Publishers
199 W. 8th Ave., Suite 3
Eugene, OR 97401

www.wipfandstock.com

PAPERBACK ISBN: 978-1-6667-5415-5
HARDCOVER ISBN: 978-1-6667-5416-2
EBOOK ISBN: 978-1-6667-5417-9

10/13/22

For Daddy—
whose memory looms
taller, wider, deeper
than the land he nurtured

For Nova and Baby—
because the earth
is borrowed
from the children

And this our life,
exempt from public haunt,
finds tongues in trees,
books in the running brooks,
sermons in stones,
and good in everything.
I would not change it.

—Shakespeare, *As You Like It*

Contents

CONTENTS

Preface

Our lives are linked with all living things, but the awareness of that interconnection seems to be unraveling, imperiling both personal and collective health. With images of devastation and violence bombarding us daily, we cannot deny that "the whole creation groaneth and travaileth in pain" (Rom 8:22, KJV). As the pandemic continues to prompt us to value spaces of healing, the earth also urges restoration, deceleration of our tracks across its face, and appreciation of what we have and the places where we live. From such awareness, the poems in this collection testify that our planet's future lies in our ability to embrace the oneness of life and to practice nonviolence toward each other, the trees, the seas, and all living beings. This stewardship obliges us to seek healing in its many forms—to take walks in the woods, to cure waters, to return the soil to its original state of health, to mend broken hearts and minds, to give justice to the oppressed. *The Medicine Woods* offers the spirit of what my grandmother sought when she ventured into the forest to find medicinal plants to heal her family—the poems emanate an imaginative ethnobotanical essence as they distill curative words in this time of disasters, diseases, and disillusionments.

Healing lies in our ability to "read" the living narratives all around us, abandoning the hierarchies that often define our lives. To read the book of the woods, for instance, is to understand that all living things have their own languages. Trees speak to us. The rivers tell stories. Water is a song. Understanding the unique voices written in creation—many of which are silenced, marginalized, and endangered—requires us to recognize the mother tongue that communicates life through nonviolence and elevates well-being, encouraging us to listen closely to "words" connected to our own existence.

To this end, *The Medicine Woods* illuminates how being fully present allows us to witness and communicate the inherent beauty of each living thing—something of its very own. Threaded with natural images, the poems are snapshots of the vegetation, the creatures, and the people within the landscape. Like the poems in *Trailing the Azimuth*, my first collection, these are also anchored in a sense of place. My home is located in the upper northeast corner of Tennessee, where the Clinch River is one of the most important rivers for freshwater mussels in the world. I *know* this river because I live deep in place. It is such connection to the land that also underlies the desire to defend it, to listen to its stories, to learn ways to heal it, and to return to the wholesome ancestral voices of the keepers.

As you read *The Medicine Woods*, reimagine the world through place and pray fresh life into the damaged earth. Then lay aside the book and find a natural space that sings to you— a trail, a front porch, an urban greenway. Notice the colors, the sounds, and the movements. Learn about others who once lived where you sit or walk. As this reconnection nurtures your body, mind, and spirit, notice the healing messages about how your life is linked to everything else that lives.

Danita Dodson

July 18, 2022
Sneedville, Tennessee

Acknowledgements

I give special thanks to the memory of my grandmother, Velva Ruth Barnard Dodson, who inspired the title and concept of this book—her fierce devotion to nature and her belief in its healing powers have always been with me. My deep gratitude goes to the Ahimsa Center at California State Polytechnic University, Pomona—especially Drs. Tara Sethia and Christian Bracho—for the inspiration in nonviolence. I am indebted to the Climate Reality Project for my training as a Climate Leader, and particularly to the Nashville Chapter and Allison Stillman. Special thanksgiving is uplifted for my family, my friends near and far, and my church at Swan Creek. I also give tribute to my homeplace of Sneedville, Tennessee, with its natural beauty and generous people. I am especially grateful to my niece, Colleen Trent, for our many inspirational conversations about healing. A special shout-out is in order to Grace Bradford, a friend and herbalist who permitted me to allude to the name of her herbal company, Allied Earth, in "Feeling the Electric Earth" and "The Water Diviner." I am beholden to my cousin Andrew Greene for his willingness to chat with me about ancestral remedies and water divining. I give a special thanks to several author-friends for their inspiration, encouragement, and endorsement of this book—Ann Shurgin, Hilda Downer, Delonda Anderson, and Edward Francisco. My heartfelt gratitude flows to all the nice folks at Wipf and Stock for bringing *The Medicine Woods* to life. I utter a profound prayer of thanksgiving to the good Lord for the grace to witness and to communicate the beauty of Creation. Finally, I give thanks to all of you, my readers—may you find inspiration to immerse yourselves in the curative forces of nature and, in turn, to help heal the places and the people where you live.

Snapshots of Woodland Well-Being

Solar Eclipse

In waxing light, the post-ecliptic woods
are serene and sonorous with mystical
kindness in the strange terrene harmonies
of katydids and sparrows, who never meet
in song and who perhaps, just like us, are
humbled by living laterally on a planet
whose comings and goings, though often
predicted, still instill wonder and fear,
as we watched the darkness pass and saw
the sun crown the moon with earthshine.

Golden beams illumine the green forest
now like a floodlight as dawn reappears,
a late-afternoon gift of newness washing
over the trees and the seas and the hearts
of all of us during this rare reawakening
as health and happiness—and promise—
pulse again from the bright song of earth.

In these moments, the whole land pauses,
bonded by an offbeat happening that urges
us to recognize there is something larger,
something more majestic and much wiser
than ourselves alight on a spinning globe.

The Morning as Bride

This morning in the early dawn,
the round moon is suspended
    like a glowing pearl
in a blooming woodland,
gracing the tree branches
    as it perches and dangles,
hanging onto evening memories.
    Not quite ready to pass
the torch to sun, it lingers
behind the gossamer-cloud veil
    that billows over the earth
like the covering of a bride—
a consort, a partner, a companion—
whose radiant face
    awaits, ready to reveal
its joy and health to the beloved us.
Yet morning breaks slowly this day,
    and the sun relegates
so that we might respect
a marvelous thing
    when we lift the veil,
    see the moon instead,
and realize that we must approach
the earth with humility and kindness,
knowing that what unexpected beauty
    the day may hold is that
    to which we are espoused,
to which we must promise ourselves.

Feeling the Electric Earth

I overturn old stones and new plants,
even risking the tangles of brambles
in my ancestors' Tennessee woods
as I seek sassafras and yellow root,
forest medicine and mountain lore,
myself a part of the allied earth.

Then before I think about it, quickly,
I reach a curious hand to the ground,
submerging it in the waves of green,
life floating in a lurid sea of vines,
and bring up a five-lined skink,
its vibrant blue tail slinking friendly
across my palm—an elongated jewel
set against the pink silk of my skin,
this delicate creature who weaves
in and out of the deepest woods,
melding with the colors of nature,
basking in sun—electric movement
in tune with the vibes of the earth.

Releasing the skink almost at once—
the way I had seen my Mamaw do
after she'd studied its essence for a bit
but then resolved it wasn't a plaything—

I decide I just must learn to master
        its precise zigzag cadence,
this delicate organic balance
            of loitering and darting,
of absorbing and releasing,
        of blending and being,
of honoring stone and cherishing soil.

Batik

Often on serene morning walks, I meet
the wild, old terrapin I've named *Batik*
because his shell and body are adorned
with spirited patterns in brown and gold,
seeming to dash and dance along the path
though his movement is quite contained—
bringing to mind how the human spirit,
too, can bounce with the liveliest tempo
even while its flesh carapace reposes.

So Batik sits immobile upon the trail
that weaves through these dense woods,
smack in the middle of where I amble
along this blue East Tennessee ridge—
and when I kneel near him in calm awe,
his yellow-mottled head and feet choose
never to withdraw into the domed shield,
his red eyes glowing knowingly bright.

Still I wonder if he feels threatened by
me, so I talk to him. *May I share these*
woods with you, Batik? I am harmless.

    Am I?

What choices will I make that somehow
will endanger his piece of wilderness?

Enigmatizing the earth he has long trod,
Batik reemerges over and over again
as I saunter oftentimes along this path,
his attachment to home pure like mine—
compelling me to consider him to be
my totem, my message, my kindred.

But I know that his reappearance here
has little—whatsoever—to do with me
because this is really his woodland
instead of my own.

Mussel Power

The clean, silver branches
of the sycamore tree overhang
the embracing banks of the old river,
their billowing leaves slowly turning
lemon yellow in the expanding light,
and walnuts cover the autumn ground,
ready food for the squirrels and us.
Here the clear shallow water runs fast
and cold over the rocky bottom
of the shoal, where the river jewels
move alive, their freshwater shells
shimmering in the refracted sunlight.

Ranging from the size of a button
to a wallet's width, small and quiet,
these creatures spend their long lives
buried partly in the riverbed sediment,
overlooked in the long fray of the day.
But their circadian work for the planet
is colossal—filtering gallons of water,
cleaning it of algae and silt and even
human impurities, restoring the health
of the river and also the well-being
of fish and frogs, plants and insects,
and all of us who depend on this flow.

Fluted Kidneyshell, Birdwing Pearly,
Snuffbox, Pleasantshell, Shiny Pigtoe—
they sound like names of rock bands,
but they are left out of the spotlight
of other more glamourous species,
though their beds like coral reefs
are clustered with jeweled diversity,
and though they foster life's motion.
Their real names should be spoken—
Community Builder, Refuge Creator,
Recordkeeper of Nature, Historian,
Water Purifier, Aquatic Hero, Healer.

For if we don't esteem them right now,
they won't be around too much longer.
Then how will a clean, pure river still
run through this place that sustains us?

The Grace of Leaves

That sliver of a silver moon
has disappeared and gone,
the earthshine dissolved like

the cosmic dust from heaven,
remnant of the nocturnal song,
and the day has broken again

with kindness in fulsome light
as tree blossoms fall like snow
in a rippling dance downward,

the postscript of a bud break,
fertile love written on a breeze,
gilt pollen and stigma awash,

the petals passing power soon
to lyrical lime-green leaves,
which will reign in the forest

for many temperate months,
a chlorophyll choir singing
from the lungs of the trees,

breathing through stomata,
a miracle of life and oxygen,
like us instinctually seeking

the vitalizing light of the sun,
affirming the grace of leaves
is also what we've been given.

Transient Art in the Gloaming

Sometimes Artist paints a jewel-tinted sky
in the gloaming as a promise that wellness
exists even in the fading shades of life.

Amethyst and ruby specters drift across
the sun-kissed vault of heaven, scattering
joy upon the murky, brown earth that melds
with the onyx sculptures of impending night—

those austere trees in silhouette on the hills,
saluting the departing sun, which waves
its hands like a child, knowing with full faith
it will return tomorrow to romp and play.

The transient art of the moment is what lies
at the palpable heart of life, like this Baroque
sky, filled both with umbra and luminance.

And the silent mysteries that will soon walk
the sunset like a stranger headed somewhere,
the obsidian garments flowing on the breeze,
will weave their way into our being like light.

The sun shall arise with healing in its wings.

Impressionist Spring

Lucent chartreuse leaves dapple the hills,
redbud stipples gleam in the spring breeze,
and joy washes the woodland in song.

Empyrean brushstrokes by the Master Hand
paint white streaks of light on the bluest sky,
and clever hatching makes green grass glow.

The earth grows and moves in benevolence
in this constantly changing creation—
Impressionist masterwork mounted within
the scraggy wooden frame of my window,
installed today in the museum of my soul.

As I watch this perpetual earthen painting,
I grow to see—I don't have to force myself
into being, into becoming. I already am—
an impasto made in light, a piece of work
dematerialized and shimmering, pulsing
from the broken-hued brilliance of the sun.

The Place I Was Born

I've always seen the place I was born
                     as a place apart.
Its remoteness
and its movement as slow as molasses
mark it as the land that time forgot,
        or the place trapped in history—
a two-redlight town in a valley
hugged by mountain mamas,
where our people
              bend and curve and glide
our vowels so elaborately
that Siri and Alexa can never find
the things we are searching for.
Our Cherokee forebears prized the earth
          here as a summer hunting place,
abundant in wildlife and forest health,
and our diverse Melungeon ancestors—
quilted from the vivid pieces
          of the planet's places—
ventured into this safe and secluded land
         that no one else seemed to want,
where we have chosen to remain
               because we do.
The place I was born gives sanctuary
to the endangered species of river life
living freely
            in a land apart,

in harmony with rare plants and birds
along the undammed water's edge,
       as apartness sings a blessing
in new songs preserved in old earth.
So I consider again—anew with pride—
this place touched by few over time,
          where I can still climb
       the three tiers of Elrod Falls,
the ropes my lifeline
as I watch the peregrine falcon
                   perch in red oak
and see my own heart alight in beauty.

Riddle of the Roan

Its name a riddle best left unanswered,
the *Roan* belies any aim to contain it.
This moniker cannot possibly embody
everything in a red highland glowing—

the fulgent wild-mountain ash berries,
the Catawba rhododendrons ablaze,
the streams once crimson by ancient war,
the anamnesis of Daniel Boone's horse,
left here to heal from a rough journey,

for nature is an enigma ensconced,
the vegetation interwoven with histories.

Though it mystifies the wanderer here
that the highland isn't really a mountain,
but a single ridgetop spanning five miles,

it does not matter—whatever one sees
on the Roan defies logic since the riddle
is the labyrinth path itself across the bald,
dis-solved simply by taking pensive steps

through dense thickets of wild blueberries
and windswept wildflowers woven into
the sun-drenched grasslands that rise up
where the blue-hazed peaks appear like

sky islands afloat in the bounding main—
the Round, the Jane, the Grassy Ridge.

Up where the Roan breathes at 6,000 feet,
the silence is so pristine and profound,
and civilization's sorrows do not intrude,
do not threaten, do not vanquish the faith
that obstacles might indeed be overcome,
traversed like the puzzled paths crossed

by the Overmountain Men, hardscrabble
pioneer-warriors who took on the massif
and sheltered at Shelving Rock overnight,
marching at dawn through the thick snow,
seeming to ask posthumously, *Traveler,*
who are you that your trials seem larger?

Smoky Mountain Memory

Beneath yellow buckeyes and silver bells,
we dip our feet in the cool rushing rapids
as the Little Pigeon River's clear flow
bathes the large rocks that seem to tumble
like fallen giants from the Chimney Tops.
Around us are the cucumber magnolias,
adopted into the diverse overstory
of the cove hardwood forest in a ravine,
their lucent leaves reflecting sunlight,
their milky flowers scenting the breeze
as salamanders sally from the stream,
weaving in and out of the moist forest,
their cheerful bodies mingling with colors
of the bee balm, jewelweed, bloodroot,
toothworts, trillium, and bleeding hearts.

And the earth here holds older memories
of when American chestnuts towered
over the misty groves where still ancient
hemlocks join more recent broadleaf trees,
and where echoes of Cherokee voices
whisper the sacred wonders of pigeons.

The flow of water over the jumbled
choreography of the morphed sandstone
invites us to rediscover the way
that we also have been formed over time—
a family of four whose love is shaped
by forces of grit and grace at work in life.

So pulled away today from life's cares,
we breathe the freshness, hold no tension,
the clean mountain air rippling across
our faces in this green paradise,
where society's sounds are waterlogged
by the force of the river's life-giving love,
flushing out all other places and faces
      but One
          as we are One,
while freedom flows over stone crevices
underneath the laced shelter of trees,
and the dance of light on water is enough.

Road to Florence

The Lombardy poplars
seem as soaring as spires,
elongated skyward
like a vertical song,
their verdant limbs dazzling
like new Venetian glass
laced with dew and sunshine,
eagerly bidding me
into the luring woods
to caper among them
to an old Tuscan tune—
if only I had time.
But onward I must move
with willful purpose through
shining sunflower fields,
gnarled olive trees, rolling
purple vineyards as I
spy old medieval towns
perched securely atop
the great gilded mountains
with silhouette sunlit
forests of ancient beech,
trees of the Abruzzo
bedizened with lichens
in the last refuge for
the Apennine wolf and
the Marsican brown bear,

extinct everywhere else.
I'm bound to sit raptly
with history awhile,
to touch old, singing stones
and testifying trees—
to hope to remember
the deep ancient longing
that drew the Etruscans
long ago to this place,
where the sun's a candle
across the verdant hills.

Monteverde

A bone-rattling dirt road winds toward
the mystifying cloud-soaked woodland
along the Cordillera de Tilarán,
where fecund layers of plants cloak
gnarled trees that stand with open arms,
exhibiting kindness as they welcome
vines and bromeliads, all epiphytes—
a natural embrace of refugees.

Forest bathing in a biodiverse haven,
I cross the bridge suspended in air
above the cloud-laced green glory
adorned with red and fuchsia flowers
that drink dew like insatiate jewels—
the orchids, the birds of paradise,
and the open-cupped neoregelia—
while somewhere in their midst lie,
still unknown, perhaps the key cures
to the earth's deadliest diseases,
healing deep in the medicine woods.

Beneath the millennia-old ficus tree,
I spend a moment with earth history,
alone with quetzals and golden toads,
where any human sounds are muffled
by spirited calls of jaguars and ocelots,

and where all the happiness one needs
is to watch the white-faced capuchins
frolic across the branch-laced ceiling.

This eco-song of Costa Rican woods
echoes the Tico blessing of *pura vida*
in a peaceful country with no army,
anchored in *naturaleza,* where schools
plant trees and where painted *carretas*
mimic the movement of forest life—
artfully devoted to keeping the earth.

Voices and Vestiges in Earth

Earth Laughter

There are healing echoes
of laughter—
      laughter—
resounding joyfully in the soil,
most opulently in springtime
when the heart quickens best,
the sonorous leap of spirit
moving with the redolent rhythm
of renewed earth and promise
as energy rises to reclaim
the frozen, forgotten dreams.

If I listen closely, I hear tones
of bliss in an awakening forest
alongside this Tennessee creek.
Cerulean warblers chirp freely,
and yellow celandine poppies
have sprawled themselves
in prolific sunny giggles,
rising diagonally up and across
the sloping ridge—bouncing,
abounding, like smiley faces
in the early-spring benevolence
amid the dry leaves of old life
and the aliveness of bees,
stemmed sunshine serenading
in newborn song, eternal youth
pulled to the surface in cheer,
inviting us to laugh and to heal.

Beech Speech

Like the other trees in the forest,
I have a tongue that speaks—
veritably recounting all year long
narratives in branches and leaves.

I'm the oft-ignored beech tree.
                    You should listen to me—

I am a storyteller of the past
and a diviner of the future,
weaving history into the present,
like folksongs with minimalist lyrics
incanted from the roots of earth.

You can learn compelling truths
from the other trees as well—
if you should stop to heed
their diverse dialects,
the lessons of their trunks,
their sagacious sighs in breezes.

But I am special and unique,
as you are special and unique.
Like you, no doubt, pilgrim,
I plead to be heard, night and day,
most often in the dead of winter.

The old leaves stay with me—
I cannot shake their lingering.
Beautifully bleached and curled,
green long gone, rattling still
in the chilly late-March wind,
they cling to my corporal twigs,
part of me, echoing my heartwood,
waving like banners to announce
that I am not quite finished,
that I am still in progress—
that we *all* are in a transient,
sentient process of becoming.

Streams and Stones

Go to a stream
as close to home as possible—
a river, a creek, a cascade,
trickling with the song of water,
a molten melody we should
never muffle or dam or ignore.

Listen to it. Be with the flow.
Feel the reminder of kinship
when you see the liquid drops
of life force running near you—

You are made of water.

Find there a small stone carved
by that same stream's course,
and carry it away to your home,
taking the time to study it closely
in the dim candlelight of evening,
discovering all
its crevices and its colors,
its shapes and its voices,
its sermons written in stone.

Allow this simple gift of earth
to tell you about what it has seen,
about the life forged by water,
about its place on this earth—
                    and Yours.

Cherish its stories of fortitude,
of the compounded beauty formed
by time, endurance, and the promise
that strata and soul will outlast
                    disasters and diseases—
will survive long past your life.

The Language of a River

To know the language of a river
is to speak with its great fluency,

to honor its most essential sounds,
to hear the uniqueness of its voice,

those transparent ripples of being
that pull rhythm to the surface,

luring us like bluegrass vocals
to layers of high lonesome peace,

where harmonies of ebb and flow
carry curing songs over the shoal.

My river has a tongue honeyed
with the ancient argot of hill folk,

the riparian idiom of my people,
its words flowing and forming

like the curves of Pygmy Madtom
beneath the waters of the Clinch,

the crown of the mountain empire,
the voice of the endangered,

with no code-switching its accent,
as unfeigned as water star-grass.

Haunted by Hollers and Hills

I am haunted by hollers and hills.
However much I wander outside
the fortressed blue-green kingdom,
      they follow me
like the *geancanach* or the *Nunne'hi*—

journeying across the broad plains
and over the steeled towers of cities,
redirecting me to the cool rivers,
singing to me of the quaint hamlets,
pocket-sized towns like Sneedville,

where the soup beans and cornbread
sit welcomingly on an inherited stove,
where the tongues of ancestors speak
still the folkways of family farms
that preserve, honor, and sustain life
as clear and pure as a jar of apple jelly.

And though I am surely a chameleon,
flitting and fitting along global paths,
leaving home and returning home,
mourning home and rejoicing home,

this is the one true place where I can
most commune with the green earth—
so that every tree I regard as I travel
evokes memories of all the trees I've
ever loved in the hollers and the hills.

Hammer Dulcimer

Hammer dulcimer,
beat out the notes of my soul
in enchanting natural ballads.
Rivet across the ancient strings
of memory and landscape
a pounding pulse,
full-toned as the deep flow
of the life-bearing Clinch River.
Sing the sounds that echo
in the whitest water ripples
over smooth, time-beaten rocks
beneath the silent shield
of the embracing hills.

Hammer dulcimer,
be my kin and blessed friend,
most beloved soulmate of place.
Render a roaring old story
of Appalachian Mountains
and twanged English,
neither of which I can
ever really put behind me.
Embrace my hill-girl ways,
whose earth-pureness exists only
in a few remote places,
where a blue-green roof
guards me when I sleep.

Touching This Mountain

One day I saw the indigo mountain,
and I rose up so sure to touch it—
      but I could not.
The outstretched fingers of my hands,
so tiny against the sculpted contours,
could not even begin
                to reach forth
then clench an entity
far too inestimable, too immanent.
I failed then to understand just why
I couldn't possibly clutch something
that was so completely embraced
by the borders of my small heart,
rounded, contained,
sheltered by love.
Still, I must cherish this mountain,
hold it closely—though inadequately—
      fight for its right to exist,
             before it is removed
from my sight,
      its contours razed.

Lizard Lore

I want you to know I remember the day
I discovered the world, the day I first saw
the grand expanse of earth around me,
the original memory, revealed in color—
that of a high mountain and a new ground
to be drudged for possibilities, wild land
no one else wanted but you, Dad, and me.

My mind-photo of a pulsing panorama,
big and bright and green, unfolded exactly
the moment you placed a moving lizard
in my three-year-old hand and said to me,
"Dear, you want something to play with?"
And, of course, I did, trusting a mother,
seeking a plaything I had never known.
It was a toy brought from another world
and another time with its long curved tail.

You wanted so much then to offer me joy,
unable to give me store-bought treasures
to feed my questing, questioning soul.
But you gave me so much more that day—
you shocked me into beholding creation.
And this first memory is so fierce that it
stings my eyes because I know—as I did
at that moment, my real moment of birth—

that life is about turning over new ground
while honoring the old, about carrying
on molting limbs the vestiges of the past.

Though now aged and weighted with time,
I realize that this lizard lore has made me,
like it once had made you, a keen-eyed seer,
charged with percipience, a child of the need
to remain at one with the rain and the desert.

I have hibernated under tree bark and earth,
but I will return one day to reclaim the sun,
to bask on clement stones—regenerated—
to examine my expanded self and reaffirm
my belonging with the everlasting creation.

Mountain Melancholy

Days of swinging grapevines
        over churning crystal creeks
are slipping into oblivion,
and unsullied recollections
of the joyful songs of countless birds
        are floating on the mountain mist,
leaving the earth and drifting
        up toward eternal green pastures
as an elegy for a way that's dying,
like the farmland and the farmers are,
whose old plows rust in forgotten fields.
To wade in those crystal creeks again,
wrapped in the honeysuckle breeze,
would be balm in these grievous times,
but so much has changed—
        as the climate has changed—
though some water still trickles
through this blue strip of hills,
and though the earth still holds some soil
in mountains ancient but ignored,
        with their mournful memories
        of chestnuts and monarchs.
It has been said *you can't go home again*,
where the unadulterated echoes
of springtime innocence and laughter
        drift along on the breeze's song.

If only we had known back in our youth
how pristine was the earth
where we walked,
how untroubled the skies.

Mariposas

Butterflies arrive with calm artistry,
brought directly to our troublesome world
on soft velvet wings and gentle whispers
that flit dreamlike into the waning sun,
sent as angelic messengers of promise
or breathless sighs of impending sorrow.

******

A few summers back, I began to feel
bizarre sensations when my car soared
through pockets of spirited butterflies
making their way across the wide highway
from one perfumed blossom to another.

Then, I began to heed my casualties.
In my rearview mirror, I saw the shards
of broken wings and disfigured bodies—
the machine in the garden destroying
with its power the bringers of visions.

******

Later, as I walked down a country lane,
a tree-lined corridor of light and peace,
I glanced at my feet, noticing my boots
within inches of two black swallowtails.

As I observed them, they took no notice,
preoccupied as they were with something
much more important—life and death.

One of them doggedly flapped its wings,
trying to lift its companion's listless sails,
plastered flat to the ground by a vehicle,
but the efforts of this Samaritan yielded
no discernible progress, no difference—
yet it didn't waver in its devoted attempt
to restore its fellow traveler, revealing
its visceral faith in the green gift of life
even as it mourned the sudden stillness.

Moved to sobs, I deliberated whether
butterflies might just know more about
compassion and love than humans do.

******

As bulldozers annihilate the forests,
and pesticides poison quaffing insects,
perhaps these flitting souls with broken
wings resurrect in broken places, sighing
just before they move on to other worlds.

So when we happen to spot a butterfly,
we do not really know where it has been,
where it might be going on its path anew,
or what special message it communicates.

Like the stunning carroty-hued monarch,
it might've travelled a very long journey,
migrating south to Tennessee mountains
on its way to the depths of Michoacán
to join the song of abundant butterflies,
each flapping wing amplified by another,
to hang in clusters to trees like a welcome,
a single trunk graced by a million wings
that wait for the sun to shine so that they
can cascade like waterfalls into light.

Summer Paradoxes

Kneeling on dry grass in the extreme heat,
I pray for rain, crying for the healing
of my scorched yard and my lifeless garden,
watching the clouds above the blue ridge,
where trees have died these past few years,
forest loss changing the nebulous shapes
that roll like mobile mountains in a race,
speaking dreams and dangers for our earth.

Then the floodgates suddenly open wide,
the trusting arid ground drinking thirstily,
without rain for these many long weeks.
But it can't swallow all, its belly gorged
with the falling sheets of endless water—
a weird weather bomb tailing a drought,
a strange cycle looping over and over
this summer like a bad horror movie.

Soon the creeks overflow their banks,
and the desiccated river is overtaken
by the fluxes that engulf the wildflowers
stranded on the banks, hiding them forever
from sun, burying them again in earth—
burying much more in Eastern Kentucky,
making me wish I hadn't prayed for rain,
bringing me to my knees again in the mud.

Next of Kin

I found him in the forest with the other slain,
casualty of violence upon the woodland kin.
And though I was squeamish at the sight,
I just could not look away from his remains
since I—one with life and breath—am liable.
Torn in half, his trunk truncated brutally,
he lay where he fell, across the troubled soil.

It was then I saw our Mother embracing him—
this soft maternal pieta, full of moss and earth,
as a deep cry resounded in the expanse of sky.
And I prostrated myself to the ground in pain,
wondering why such suffering continues.

With the courage to come closer, I kneeled
to pay my last respects, caressing the frazzled
strips of skin, then noticing the wood cells,
the history of one being's time on the planet,
the missing stories of a shortened life—and
I cried too with our Mother, seeing how long
he had stood in the forest, this lignified leader
whose leaves will no longer grace the green
days of the woodland and speak holy wisdom.

So I, as next of kin, reconnected and reunited,
must exit the forest to seek my vengeance,
to cry reality and release these sealed truths
to those who deny deforestation and violence
have anything to do with them—who do not
see the relationship between *kind* and *kin*.

Ecology for Eli

The earth recollects his fleeting spirit here,
though no one else has until now, this ghost
of a Union recruit left behind in a hospital
at Soldier's Cave in the Cumberland Gap—
sick, stranded, scared in a blue-gray valley
of dried bones and demoralizing famine,
where mountains held sardonic earthworks
in an East Tennessee ripped violently in two
by merciless muskets and leaden loyalties,
where a teenage boy could be conscripted
to later disappear from the rock-riven hills.

Eli's story certainly wasn't unique in a war
upon soldiers, civilians, and countryside,
the disunion and the damage scarring all,
ecological catastrophe of the first degree,
deep destruction of the land and the heart—
as Sherman cut a broad swath of earth
on his march to the sea, devouring forests,
as Sheridan led a scorched-earth crusade
through the Shenandoah Valley, following
the call to *eat out Virginia clear and clear.*

Trees were massacred—about two million—
armies axing them for firewood and bridges,
destroying the habitats of birds and bats,

the roots of life shattered, ravaged, stolen.
The trees left standing often bore their own
battle scars, *perfectly riddled with bullets.*

And Eli, riddled with his own pain in the Gap,
a gardener and a lover of green wholeness,
a singer of psalms of peace and joy, watched
the birds in flight and fright like himself,
his homeplace nowhere now but in memory,
so he left the cave as Kirby claimed the Gap,
finding a brave new world, a dystopia awash.

Bounteous fields were stripped bare, leaving
behind a truncated landscape—a wasteland—
a mournful reality that Thoreau had termed
a *war with the wilderness,* the imprint of hate
chiseled and impounded upon flesh-like soil.
Minerals were mined for violence, conflicts
changing the shape of the land, depressing
and paining the earth with grisly cruelty,
leaving festered sores for thousands of miles—

while someplace in the East Tennessee woods,
Eli fell prey to the famine, the food injustice,
and the fear of being outcast and unloved,
and facedown he lay dreaming of healing,
of finding herbs and heart again to be whole.

And as forests vanished, the earth warred back,
with its insects and mosquitoes, and afterwards
a few good souls began to plant seeds of change,

the visionaries of a movement to preserve
what was left, speaking for the vanquished trees,
voicing a word that rose like dawn—*ecology*.
It was a type of redemption—a healing begun.

Though Eli rests among hemlocks somewhere
between Gap Cave and Big Creek, his bones
never recovered, his story only now spoken,
these words sing justice for both past and future,
chaunting the truth that chasms in humanity
create corresponding clefts in the earth.

The Healing Landscape

To see the world from the mountain peaks,
a bird's eye vista like we nature lovers
esteem, is to view only the mere vestiges
of the epic wildness that once was there.

Even so, we honor and love these remnants
because we are awed by their sublimeness,
because our instinct shows us that they can
give voice to the forgotten words living

boldly in their vast storehouse of wisdom—
the trees and water, the loam and stone,
holdings in an ancient terrigenous library,
written in curative languages still new to us,

their strange earth tongues speaking healing
beneath the surface, lilting subatomic truths
that take time and care to translate well
since the particles add to All and to One.

These preserved pieces of landscape apprise
us with a sanative blessing that overturns
the shams and the fury of a pandemic world,
its stresses and diseases and anger and hate,

allowing us to stand above it all—restored.

Meditations for Healing

Mid-Morning Meditation

The gifted grace of green things utters
good health from the rising heart of life,
calm like a mid-morning meditation
with rounded mala beads rolling across
the singing fingers of gratitude.

This day there is no buckwheat cushion
in a Zen-graced corner of a warm room.
Today mindfulness walks in the woods.
So still in the forest, I pause and stand,
bathing myself in the sounds of cicadas
after making that most spirited stride
into splendid nothingness to welcome
the copious somethingness of the wild.

This is the turning time of mid-morning
when the sun appears like a gentle tap
just before swift movement of creatures
wipes away cobwebs of evening's work,
when the small insects still flit and flap
wondrously in the leaf-filtered sunlight,
when the breeze that carries everything
passes by with the voice of life a-breath.

Nothing could be sweeter this morning
than to claim presence in a living space,

where I'm written into an agrestal canvas
outside society's clangor and fracas,
where I find well-being
is just *being* here.

Breathing Scotland

The breath draws slowly inward,
much like the sea's ebb, pulling
backward to allow the sand
enough space to meet the sun,

who caresses its soft face
with flow of winnowing light
in bounden energy
in the morning's briskness

as a castle grows upward,
its tall molten spire grazing
the top of the universe
just before the rising wall

collapses and deconstructs
as the tide's respiration
rushes forth with sound and spate,
immersing life and the day
in the liquescent outbreath

honored at this kindred space,
where Scotland's old sea beckons
the clean kinship of new earth,
like a story unfolded
in a lilting *cèilidh* dance.

An Angler Aloft

There is a river,
a wellspring of being,
  where I fish
    for words,
an angler aloft,
  atop the streams
of experiences
  and memories,
seeking perhaps
    a snippet
of moving life
that can be caught,
  its slick surface
touched but briefly,
  its beaded eyes
shining in reflection
    of knowing,
until I throw it back
  to live, to be a part
of an organic flow—
of an original form—
  of Creation,
  of Creativity.

Canticle to the Creator

Wherever I look on this planet,
    beautiful and warped,
    triumphant and limping,
    fused and fragmented,
    restored and un-mended,

I see You in

    the flow of the creeks,
    the sun-kissed gardens,
    the lichen in the forests,
    the arrival of mountain laurel,
    the sending of rain,
    the starkness of sandstone,
    the slenderness of aspens—

one blade of grass,
one speck of dust,
one branch of maple,
one petal of dogwood,
one sigh,
one cry—

all sounds,
    all shapes,
all places,
    all faces,
all seeing,
    all being—

You are Creation.
    You are Creator.
You make a way
    out of no way—

springing seeds to life,
    sculpting canyons,
        pouring waterfalls,
            painting deserts.

La Embraza del Creador

High atop a mountain above
the Masaya Volcano,
the long arms of a giant cross reach,
a remote symbol in a stark landscape,
but its placement here
causes the mind to soar
outward, upward, downward
to seek the holy message that speaks
across miles and miles,
                 plunging to the pits
of the sculpted canyons,
scaling the spire-like summits,
                 gliding
across streams, rivers, and seas,
enfolding cities, countries, continents,
bridging together the broken segments
of humanity that God somehow
determines still to embrace.
A reminder of the impossible possibility
                 of a planetary renewal
came on a poignant day ages ago
when the massive weight
of an ancient tree thudding,
                 thudding,
against the ground in dramatic rhythm
was replanted in the unforgiving soil
         with Forgiveness upon it,

whose arms   extended Love
to a world filled with hate.
And the globe shuddered in unison.
And the earth quaked in every corner.
And all merged in a strange moment
of synchronous tragedy and hope.
On other days since then when
we intuit this impossible possibility—
when we sense that these arms enfold
                    the universe in unity,
amid our crushing fears and sufferings—
we feel reconciled to the Creator
                    and to each other,
reconciled also to all living things,
singing empathy from soil to sky,
understanding we are meant to extend
the same embracing (( )) love.

Holy Trees

In these old, wood-pulp pages, I see
a bright, green, and varied trail of trees—
      to the Revelation from the Genesis.

Heroes and villains live in the sentences,
but the trees are what capture me most,
speaking with golden tongues in trunks,
bearing truths with vocal cords in roots.

The story is an ancient one—
      God, trees, and humans.
The Oxygen. The Breath.

The Tree of Life—the sublime Divine—
is the mother tree that links and sustains
all trees planted by the Green Gardener.
And the Tree of Knowledge is a narrator,
revealing all the truths of life and death,
drawing to it humans who know little.

Hence, they're banished from the Garden,
      and they and their kind ever after
look for the shades and flavors of trees,
their whispers and their strengths,
seeking their wisdoms and their lessons,
seeing in their branches the shape of God
and the wonders of mighty possibilities—

to hear the marching in mulberry trees
and the voice of Being in a bush afire,
to meet the All by the old oaks of Mamre,
to sweeten Marah's waters with bark,
to offer Forgiveness incarnate upon a tree.

Reading holy trees—Wood and Word—
I, too, imagine I Am a fruitful bough
by a well with branches overflowing a wall,
sapwood and pith, life force and knowledge,
a woman as bold as Deborah, who has found
her voice, her people, and her justice under
a tree where birds nest, my story interwoven
with theirs,
    this poem a palm branch.

Birthright

Morning breaks in an autumn valley
as clouds hover in an upside-down brine
cast over the amber and hennaed hues
of the alchemizing mountains, gleaming
like a mirror's reflection behind a curtain.

Here belonging lies within the *caim*,
these quilted hills casting a circle
of braided prayer around me, a refuge
of community where I am safe and loved—

even in this dark time of loss and pain,
even in this sorrow of being newly orphaned,
where I can see with the eyes of the owls,
move with the growth of the trees, and
sense my parents in the mountains' breath.

For one word whispers and penetrates
the fire-bitten force of the fall frost—
one word rising from an archaic voice.

Dúcas. Birthright. Inheritance. Place.

My heritage probes the surface images,
just like the sun behind these clouds,
seeking again the soul-atmosphere
that seeped into me the instant I first awoke

as a newborn in this circle of wilderness
to which my belonging was destined—
blessed to me the wide sky above me,
blessed to me the green grass beneath me,
blessed to me the loved ones around me.

Given. Passed on. *Ag fillead ar do dúcas.*
Like new rainwater in an old, wooden barrel,
I am linked forever to the ancient earth,
compassed by the medicine woods, keeping
peace and health within the braided circle.

This Frame of Spirit

I am a crumbling
skeletal mess,
    a heap of bones
stoppable and breakable,
aging branches and limbs
of a body now fragile,
a catabolic sack of cells
slowly returning
to the loam and to the ether,
accepting transient life.

But this frame of spirit
will live in earth again,
will weave into flowers,
will sing in a new way
the fullness
of all possibility,
        as it flows
into Creation,
    as it merges
with Source,
released skyward
as dust and minerals
    wafting in light,
fused to Breath.

The Roundness of Being

Oh, Stunning Planet—
our inspiring, spheric home—
you mystify us with your nocturnal,
ebony ceiling damascened by diamonds
at the end of the day, and you uplift with an
azure canopy when the halcyon daystar shines,
generously singing an eternal song as we spin ever
diurnally eastward on the constantly moving ground,
soaring aloft like an eagle easy in the arc of existence,
dumbstruck by the metamorphosing mystery above us
in an open awning—the Sky Vault of Cherokee lore,
to which this domed domicile is attached, a cupola
hanging over us like an overturned blue teacup,
its libation pouring upon the earth and all its
creatures equal portions of life-laced air,
daily gracing us anew with rhythms
of moonlight and sunlight and
the roundness of being.

Shabbat

Shabbat, holy sublime,
creation at time-out,
a space—a pace—
        separated
from the fray of the day,
pulling back from labor
to pronounce everything
in these golden hours
        Good—
this restoration,
this rest as resistance,
this breath of repose,
this season of fallow—
        an intermission
from dramas and traumas
to look in the mirror
of bright attendance
and see the natural healing
that whispers in the pines,
that sings in the soil,
that laughs in the hills.

Dance of Winter and Spring

Slanting snow now blows
white on white blossoms,
winter and spring swirling
in a wild and lyric samba
against the darkening sky
and the silhouetted curves
of purple-gray mountains—
a yin-yang whirligig created
from nature's sidestepping.

That dividing line between
tombs and open spaces
is like a binary tightrope
that wrestles moon and sun
to balance essential forces
within the soil and the sea,
within the roots and the sky,
weaving Piscean movement
into the lives of all things,
                    Being afloat,

and the day's taut equipoise
could be counted as grace—
the reminder that the earth
gambols in its own rhythms,
inviting us to the wild steps
we can barely begin to dance.

Dogwood Ahimsa

To sit fixed in the sacred stillness
of the shadows in the early bright
is to honor the clean slate of life,
the viridity in the day's beginning,
a fluid movement of mind singing
gracefully like a new earth gesture,
the Prithvi Mudra of rising dawn,
weaving sunrise into open soul.

This act of being ever so present
and conscious of all that speaks life
is to breathe in the spirit of *ahimsa*,
to mindfully embrace nonviolence—
an intent akin to watching with care
the flowering dogwood abloom.

In the snowy blossoms of this tree,
through the blood-marked petals,
the earth has absorbed the violence
moving through its soil and roots,
the muck of ancient antagonisms
sown by humanity throughout time,

then transformed into compassion
every cry of pain, every act of hate,
every cut tree, every slain body,
every mother's grief—
                    calling us

to remember the earth's wounded
and to see each petal as a message
not only of the deepest sufferings
but also of nonviolence reclaimed,
the wholeness and the dayspring
that we protect like sentinels on
                    watchtowers,
as we shield under our kind wings
everything that is threatened today.

Disciplining Naughty Children

Spin, spin, cold blizzard wind.
Swathe this limping planet.
Conceal our gargantuan footprints,
like Wite-Out on big-inked mistakes,
erasing our sweeping destruction.
Remove us from the mountains
of discarded plastic in our backyards,
the charred ruins of the old forests,
and the apathy hardened in our hearts.

Today the wind's mighty, howling voice
shrieks wildly in a solemn ritual,
drawing us toward the hidden, tired soil
that screams right now to be revivified
by the kind seeds that we might plant.

As echoes of the toxin troposphere
join the muffled cries of tainted ground
during these frozen, straitjacketed hours,
        we are barred from intervening—
we are banished from writing ourselves
on this sacred, silent tabula rasa,
so we just gaze out of ice-glazed panes
as the universe's avenging forces timely
amend our neglect of this holy ground.

Mother Earth has given her cold children
time-out today, put us under house arrest,
censored all our silver exhaust machines,
slapped our hungry, naughty-child hands
with the frostbite reproof of tough love.

And just for this reflective spell of time
in these shivering and frightening hours,
we cannot burn, cannot scar, cannot trash
her seemingly sparkling, pure-snow face,
calling us to rewrite her future—and ours.

Faces of the Poorest and Weakest

Whenever I am weighed down with burdens,
I have been taught that I should get beyond
my own petty concerns and meditate with love
          upon the *face of the poorest and the weakest,*
an act that will quickly dissolve my own being
into the Oceanic Circle of All that contains me.

This shouldn't be hard to do since everywhere
          the groans of creation resound mournfully
from the heights and depths, lengths and widths,
of the planet, ebbing and rising in continuous tides,
          these faces of suffering that I cannot ignore.

There is unspeakable desolation written there—
          farmworkers poisoned by toxic pesticides,
          families diminished by opioid addiction,
          animals slain by brutal exsanguination,
          women trafficked for profit as sex-slaves,
          children murdered in elementary schools . . .

The face of the earth itself is poor and weak—
          coral reefs bleached and their beauty effaced,
          glaciers melting from the intensifying heat,
          coastlines crowded, with no space for joy,
          seas stained with the surging blood of oil,
          rainforests on the verge of becoming savannas . . .

Afterthoughts of entropy fall into our lives,
all occurring more frequently and intensely,
coming earlier and leaving later than before—
    floods, fires, tornadoes, quakes, hurricanes,
        famine, war, racism, disease, poverty . . .

Visages of pain are many in a pleading earth,
    engulfed in consuming flames and bad water,
    buried under fallen trees and gross inequities—
images that sadly contradict the vital energy
we see in the shapes of trees and waterfalls.

Holding these faces of suffering in our thoughts,
with the radiance of sun and the tenderness of breeze,
we must pray healing, dream healing, weave healing,
speak healing, paint healing, write healing,
    bring healing back into the soil and soul.

Keepers

One Last Mountain

In the kindness of a mid-March breeze,
with the gentle rays of sun at our backs,
we journeyed together
              to Gobbler's Knob,
you moving slowly, steadily,
                    behind me,
daring to remember the rolling hills
your own parents had long ago roamed—
a trail into nostalgia, a link to stories
written in the roots of earth and family,
              the paths going higher
into belonging and keeping.

Though you rested under a tree or two
along the way, agreeing easily with me
after I begged you to stay put and wait
while I scaled our inherited mountain,
              when I looked back,
                    you were there with me,
unwilling to miss a thing of these woods,
              reconnecting yourself to place,
              teaching me how to be connected.

Then at the summit, beholding in awe
the ridges and valleys below us,
as our four green eyes reflected beauty
              all around us, all within us,

glorying in a glimpse of heaven here,
we linked ourselves—
        our hearts, our bloodline—
in a prayer of thanks
for our lives well-lived,
for the good green ground we have trod,
        for each other—
father and daughter, kin and friends.

Afterward, I followed you trustingly
        down the steep mountain slope,
boots trying to take hold in old leaves,
        embracing trees as we went,
embracing all that holds us to this life,
as I watched your 85-year-old self
recognize then not just what it is—
        but what it once was
                and what it will soon be.

Though I grasped surely that your days
were numbered—
        and that you, my hero,
could not live always and forever here—
I never imagined that one month later
you would pass from these blue hills.

When I found you in the April gloaming—
just feet away
        from the door to your home
at the end of your day nurturing the land,

the sun dipping behind the ridgeline—
    you were lying upon the earth,
cold and still,
        your kind heart shattered.
But from those eyes as green as the grass
flowed the glowing gaze of pure peace
from a sight of wonder I cannot yet know.

I've come to understand that this last day
you looked down from
        Another Mountain,
grander than you'd ever scaled before,
then you blended into clouds and wind,
into water and soil—
        into everything.

What I have left is a promise to keep—
that I'll remain connected to this land.

In memory of my father, Alfred Clarence Dodson (1936–2022)

Medicine Woods and Monkey Wrenches

When I was a child, curious and restive,
it was a Granny Woman who guided me
into the mystic woods for the first time,
where everything of the earth is an ally.
Enveloping my tiny-girl hand in hers—
her parchment skin stretched delicately
over palm and fingers like a paper glove
or an explorer's map with long rivers—
my native scout gave me forest lessons.

She named all the signs of life we saw—
beech and bloodroot, sumac and 'sang—
her visual lectures turning abruptly aural
when she noted the echoes of woodsongs,
teaching me to identify the sweet call
of the yellow warbler as she spoke about
the captive canary in Aunt Ethel's house.
"Pity the caged bird," she said, sighing,
then turned her hazel-green eyes toward
the poplar, the pine, and the peace.

And if ailments seized my frail body,
this Appalachian folk doctor foraged
the medicine woods along Swan Creek,
returning with roots and herbs in hand,
taking from the earth only that needed.
Like she'd quilted the Monkey Wrench,

weaving the truth of healing into cotton,
she secured anew what'd been loosened,
concocting teas of feverweed and cedar,
brewing sassafras root to heal the blood,
humming old hymns like it was Sunday.

I believed in her magic all along, for she—
my grandmother—was larger than life,
towering above me like an herbal myth,
a scroll from another world, another day,
who in the ancient earth of the Cherokee
carried a lucky shamrock from the *Arsh*,
bending the gold clock of Father Time,
embracing the old truths of Mother Earth,
believing in the healing power of God.

As I watched her, I grew to understand
the palliative poetry written in the soil,
where memories grow roots in the soul.

In memory of my paternal grandmother,
Velva Barnard Dodson (1914–95)

The Ballad of Biophilia

In her outpost Appalachian cabin,
she reads the universe in a pinecone,
firm faith in the dispersion of seeds—
the message that living things propagate
even amid chaos and violence.
With the commission of keeping the land
entrusted to her, she moves like a ranger,
guarding the oldest paths in the earth.

Rising before dawn to meet the dayspring,
she cherishes the fleeting resplendence
of sunrises and flowers and queen bees,
weaving her way into the day alive,
knowing it's the Now that must be kept too,
so she imbibes it well—sees the blessing—
because a good future is hinged upon
a happiness that is sustainable.

In passing, she speaks to deer and raccoons,
kindly transposing them out of harm's way,
nursing them like a mother tree that holds
the woods together, forming kinships with
all kinds of beings, the wounded and whole,
following sparrows and seedlings, singing
all the blessed while, knowing that there is
no wholeness without the music of the earth.

Ansel

Keeper of the Wild, through the wide lens
    would that I could
    limn the earth as you do
with your camera and tripod,
    entering the old-growth forest,
    dancing with the rugged and remote,
    hiking across parlous mountain passes,

fully alive in those wilderness places
where the earth and its community of life
are untrammeled by humans—
    healing spaces we know now
because of your efforts to keep them.

At one with the power of the landscape,
captivated by nature's most beautiful moments
    in the open skies of national treasures,
    you *still* draw our consciousness
toward pureness and possibility,

toward creation that counters destruction—
    flowing patterns of Canyon de Chelly,
    primal gesture of sky in the Tetons,
    clearing of a winter storm in Yosemite,
    autumn dawn in the Smoky Mountains.

Who else could—in black and white—embody
    the movement of clouds over canyons,
    the textured wood and bark of trees,
    the rainbow refracting off waterfall mist,
    the chlorophyll life of lustrous leaves?

So climb atop Helios to touch the eloquent light,
and instantiate the magic of the earth—
    sunrise and moonrise,
    oaks and saguaros,
    sand dunes and rivers,
    summits and passes—

and we will follow beauty through your lens
    until we see it through our own.

Solar Mothers

Las Mujeres Solares de Totogalpa lift
arms of indigenous strength, wielding
Women's superpower in Sabana Grande.

Keeping place in a highland savanna,
which Chorotegan stories name the land
ensconced *in the nest of the birds*,

the mystic mountain mamas are sunlit—
sustainable guardians of the solar flame,
transformers of their backwoods village.

Bathed in silver light, they bear torches
of communal creativity as they labor
with saws and hammers, building hope

from zinc and wood, their ovens of sun
saving their days of baking and cooking,
their lungs no longer engulfed in smoke,

their arms and legs now pardoned from
collecting firewood in the remote hills,
making The Women land protectors too,

now halting pollution and deforestation,
conserving Nicaraguan nature with love,
teaching and cooperating with their men,

who are landmine survivors and farmers
of the soil that holds the imprint of battle,
where much of the civil war was staged.

Though they once lived in total darkness,
The Women manifest a photovoltaic dream,
their panels ferrying celestial light to earth,

like the unfolding of an ancient prophecy,
which connects technology and antiquity—
the future held in their own present hands.

The Defenders

The Defenders are keepers of the land,
guardians on this maimed spinning globe,
lights in the darkness of slain forests
and the murky depths of polluted waters.

Their heroic actions grace our days—
as they seek to restore the roots of old land,
protect the health of mountains and creeks,
undo the violence of bulldozers and profit.

Guarding life, they risk their own.

They desire the clear gem of a whole earth—
the authentic, natural heart of the Creation—

not the diamonds in the killing fields,
not the coal in the Appalachian hills,
not the logs in the indigenous forests,
not the oil in the ocean beds,

but the air we all have a right to breathe,
the water we all have a right to drink,
the mountains that should always remain,

so the Defenders stand at Standing Rock,
and they sit at Fairy Creek,
and they walk at Boxtown,
for their civil disobedience is earth medicine.

Two Fish and Five Loaves

I saw him arrive from the Tiberias Lake,
the waves conveying him in a bark of light
into this harbor of wantonness and disease,
into this place of injustice and leprosy—
no sanctuary where anchors held any hope
until Love itself walked ashore in the form
of a fisher king who outstretched his arms
to heal with hands that didn't bear flasks
of frankincense, holy oils, or forest herbs.
The anointing was his words, pure spirit,
graced with hope, seasoned with kindness,
working miracles in the raw matter of life
as he intoned psalms and moved mending
fingers over sodden beings with ripe flesh,
we who were already returning to the soil.

But we wanted more than bodily healing,
anchored by words of change he uttered,
a new song of redemption alive like trees,
life flowing in our limbs again, reconciled.
My new gait drew me to hike a mountain
as I had never before done my whole life,
my twisted leg straightened, and my heart
as light as my feet on a trail I marched
because he'd retired to the hills to breathe
sun into the wilted plants and cloudy sky.

This morning I'd left home with my bread
and two tilapia, just enough to sustain me
for this day I'd spend listening in the grass
to his teachings on servitude and love—
the bread of life to restore a harmed world,
the inspiration to protect it, to love it all.

His words making me feel I'd run a race,
and weary as well from the morning walk,
I opened my basket and looked with thanks
at the two fish and five small bread loaves.
Then I glanced around the sprawling field,
and sitting there amid the bright anemones
were five thousand beings aglow—
dressed in rags, worse for wear than mine,
their unbathed bodies reeking with sweat.
Some had been sleeping on the streets—
I recalled their faces there. Often having
seen them hungry for food, I had limped
toward them with a few fish my father
had caught in the lake that very morning
and the bread that my mother had made.

Because giving was nothing new to me,
and now that I had received everything,
I rushed to the disciple with my basket,
offering the two fish and the five loaves,
no longer my food but belonging to all,
full of faith that the little I had mattered.
And the kind hands of the Miracle Maker,
with great compassion for food justice,
then multiplied barley bread and tilapia

into a feast for a multitude of humans,
filling them with awe as well, reminding
us of all the other daily miracles, some
of grains and meat, others of kind action.

As I watched our prayers for daily bread
materialize with this distributive love,
I fathomed the miracle of transformation
that comes when we're willing to be part
of God's life-giving plan to nurture others.

Water Keepers

Like a traveler passing Paddan-Aram,
drawn toward some dreamed purpose,
I arrive at a deep well in an arid field
just as a community is going to water.
This stream alive in the rocky ground
is cached with a stone to keep it pure,

protected from malice and pollution,
a source encircled by the thirsty sheep
and laboring humans worn for wear,
native dwellers in this humble place
that I do not really know all that well,
but one I claim as connected to me—

this place of indigenous stewardship,
where I witness the strong connection
the people have with water and land,
which they hold not as commodities
but as relatives, alive and kin to them.
Eager to be a water keeper like them,

I—a wanderer at home where I alight—
remove the heavy stone myself to help
free the water drawn then with great care
and distributed to all here with great joy,
given as freely to sheep as to humans.
As we together offer thanks for water,

I watch the drops cupped by tin ladles,
drinking the earth made a celebration,
as the aqueous echo rings straight to sky
the creative power, the sustaining truth—
that water is life and should be free
and plentiful for all, and right on time.

Foot Washer

Winding a long white linen around her waist,
she sees it trail the ground like a holy scarf
as she kneels before an ivory enamel basin
rimmed with a simple red line, where water
ripples against it like rain in a thirsty valley.

Slowly she takes the bare feet of the woman
sitting meekly on the crimson-padded pew,
whose path in life she can never fully know,
and she mindfully washes away layers of dirt
and the grimed pain of a day, a year, a life.

She honors this pair of feet in front of her
as though they were her very own—loved—
oblivious now to any dividing line between
where the water ends and her tears begin,
seeing her own face mirrored in the basin.

Though next year before her there will be
yet another pair of feet—yet another life—
it is this year and this day that count,
all that both of them have been promised,
so she awaits the moment when cleansing

will compassionately grace her own feet,
these feet that have walked the hard earth,
returning to this ritual every year because

it is her identity—the empathy of water.
For she's a Foot Washer, and an Aquarius,

whose *soul like a watered garden* remains
connected to this old and kind ceremony,
knowing that water is sacred and shared,
breathing healing to her with grace alive
like a person whose feet she has washed.

The Water Diviner

Walking over the green grassy ground
laced with red clover and dandelion,
    a swatch of earth not valued
    for its beauty or for its soil,
still he feels the electricity dance
on the forked stick in his old, worn hands,
one branch in each, held with both palms
        turned toward himself,
while the Y of the branch points
skyward, angling forty-five degrees.

Divining the earth, he water-witches,
pacing back and forth over tired land
to find the deep stream bubbling like hope
beneath the hard impossible dirt,
this preacher who sees connection
between the sweet water he discovers
and the ancient scriptures he shares—
    the Being and the Blessing,
    the Word and the Water.

With the deep faith of his elders,
who have entrusted him with this skill,
he walks with a holy charge—
    the mission of water—
    praying and waiting
until the end of the Y is galvanized
downward to the Stream and the Source.

This water, he knows, is surely a gift—
a healing force alive in the sod—
and he is just a conduit for the Hands,
    walking towards liquescence,
    resurrecting the allied earth,
baptizing the land and the people anew.

The Ancestors

From a plot of ground on a family farm,
from a story written in an inherited bible,
from a walk in an undisturbed woodland,
from many spaces and places on earth,
the voices of our ancestors hasten us
to preservation because the future
will not exist in a vacuum but must be
linked to a remembrance of the past.

The wind and the trees and the creeks
prompt us to hear the restorative echoes
of the gray-haired wisdom-keepers
of the land wherever it is we each live,
whatever heritage we carry within us—
they who left their footprints in the soil,
their prayers for us in the mountain dells,
their nurturing legacies in the flowers.

Their voices move like *Achachilas*—
ethereal mountain spirits connecting
themselves to the right weather for crops,
praying for rain or sun in the seasons,
safeguarding the lives of descendants,
appearing in dreams like wise old men
who descend their cave dwellings
in the hills to convey folk-wisdom.

Their stories float like *Pachamama*—
fertile essence of woodland ground,
life force encompassing all that is,
allowing time and space to envelop
an earth that produces and sustains,
that contains each historical event,
the principle of nature that recycles
life from death, and death from life.

Their songs rise like *Granny Women*—
healers of maladies great and small,
blending Ulster and Cherokee beliefs
to provide healthcare for the rural poor,
sharing what gifts they've inherited—
like grinding the yellow root for colic,
blowing out the fire on a burned arm,
and stopping blood with bible verses.

Touched by grace and quiet beauty,
inspiring a responsible way to live well,
their voices rise in hymns of celebration,
in prophecies of coming disasters,
in speeches of resistance to wrongs,
in prayers of thanksgiving and praise
to the Spirit that binds the human soul
to the natural world for just a little while.

What we learn from them will make us
            the ancestors one day.

Rebuilders

Like Haggai spoke to Zerubbabel
and to the fraught remnant,
bearing the sacred message
of restoration and healing,

we must *speak* to rebuild

that which is in disarray,
not only the crumbled foundations
of forgotten communities
and destroyed pieces of earth
but also the fortifications of spirit,

the grace glory reestablished
after the injustice and the violence
are cleared away to make bare
the pure authenticity in the ruins

and to give health-giving words
to lost sounds and buried voices,
this act of creative resurrection born
from the knowledge of kindness,
from the awareness that all are kin.

The call to return, to be reconciled
to place and essential being, sings
from shared cells moving within us,

the desire to build some memorial
from bricks and mortar that will last
because they are living stones—

because *we* are also living stones.

We

Living in dissonance, oblivious
to our part in the grander ecosystem,

We are that dust in the wind,
    that fragile freedom afloat,

heedless of the impact of our choices,
ignominiously unmindful of the fact

that a single cup of morning coffee
could equal the death of a songbird,

that one-third of the food supply
is wasted, uneaten, while people starve,

that fast fashion becomes fast castoffs
that the homeless could've gladly worn,

that jettisoned plastics could establish
residence in landfills for generations,

to be unearthed by beings like WALL-E,
left as primary sources of who *We* were—

when what *We* could have left behind
was a green forest or a clean stream.

We forget the truth that *We* are nature,
entangled evermore in its movements,

concatenated with each other as well
in ways *We* can only begin to fathom.

We are travelers here, ambling adrift,
strangers on an earth created as a home

We have borrowed from our children—
their place—which will diminish daily

if *We* do not keep it well,
        if *We* do not keep each other well.

Notes

Solar Eclipse

This poem refers to the Great American Eclipse on August 21, 2017.

Batik

The Eastern Box Turtle (Terrapene carolina), the official state reptile of Tennessee, is a peaceful creature that lives 30-100 years. Thriving in a natural forest habitat filled with dense leaf cover, it has a strong connection to its place of birth, never venturing far and revealing an amazing homing sense. It is classified as a "vulnerable" species, one that faces a high risk of extinction in the wild, due to habitat fragmentation and destruction as well as illegal collection.

Mussel Power

Freshwater mussels are critical to the larger ecosystems around them, but they are one of the planet's most imperiled species. Where I live, in the upper northeast corner of Tennessee, the Clinch River is one of the most important rivers for freshwater mussels in the world, with 46 different species, more than all of Europe. However, in recent years, nearly 90% of mussels here have mysteriously and alarmingly died off.

Transient Art in the Gloaming

The last line is a paraphrase of Mal 4:2 (KJV).

The Place I Was Born

The portion of the Clinch River flowing through Hancock County, Tennessee, has never been dammed. Considered the only ecologically intact headwaters of the Tennessee River system, it is named as the one river in the United States worth protecting due to its diversity of life, and it is penned as one of the "Last Great Places."

Riddle of the Roan

Straddling the North Carolina/Tennessee border, Roan Mountain is vast, wide, and stunning. More than a single mountain, it spans five summits, clad in a dense and diverse stand of spruce-fir forest, including the world's largest natural rhododendron garden and the longest stretch of grassy bald in the Appalachians. The Appalachian Trail traverses most of the Roan's crest.

Smoky Mountain Memory

The title echoes the song "Smokey Mountain Memories," written by Earl Thomas Conley. Salamanders are found in the greatest numbers and diversity in the Appalachian Mountains. The Great Smoky Mountains, known as the "Salamander Capital of the World," boasts 30 species, some of them existing nowhere else on earth. The Cherokee named the Little Pigeon River after the passenger pigeons once there but now extinct.

Road to Florence

The Marsican brown bear is a protected species found exclusively in central Italy. The Apennine wolf, the national animal of Italy, is also protected.

Monteverde

An epiphyte is a plant that grows on another plant but is not parasitic, such as the numerous ferns, bromeliads, air plants, and orchids growing on tree trunks in tropical rainforests.

Streams and Stones

The phrase "sermons written in stones" is an adaptation of a line from Shakespeare: "And this our life, exempt from public haunt, finds tongues in trees, books in the running brooks, sermons in stones, and good in everything" (Duke Ferdinand, *As You Like It*, Act 2.1).

The Language of a River

The Pygmy Madtom (*Noturus Stanauli*) is known only to exist in the Clinch River at Frost Ford and Brooks Island in Hancock County, Tennessee, and the Duck River in Humphreys County, Tennessee. It is rare and protected as an endangered species.

Haunted by Hollers and Hills

The *geancanach* is a Scots-Irish spirit of Ulster. The *Nunne'hi* are spirit people in Cherokee mythology.

Lizard Lore

This poem is based upon a story that my father shared about his first memory. Here I retell it, using his voice spoken to his mother, a woman of the woods.

Mountain Melancholy

American chestnut trees, up to 100 feet tall and 9 feet around, once blanketed the eastern forests of the United States. Then a deadly blight spread, killing 4 billion trees within 40 years. Mountaintop removal due to surface coal mining occurs primarily in eastern Kentucky, southern West Virginia, southwestern Virginia, and eastern Tennessee. A study in 2009, commissioned by Appalachian Voices, showed nearly 1.2 million acres had been surface mined for coal, destroying more than 500 mountains. I use "*you can't go home again*" from the title of a Thomas Wolfe novel.

Mariposas

"Mariposas" is Spanish for "butterflies," a nod to the inspiration of a passage about butterflies in Gabriel Garcia Marquez's *One Hundred Years of Solitude*. Over the past four decades, more than 450 butterfly species have declined rapidly by nearly 2 percent a year, due to warmer autumns in the western United States (Forister, M.L. et al. "Fewer Butterflies Seen by Community Scientists

Across the Warming and Drying Landscapes of the American West." *Science*, vol. 371, 6533 [2021]: 1042-1045).

Summer Paradoxes

Like the ecological whiplash experienced in Eastern Kentucky in late July 2022, the vicious cycle of droughts and floods is fueled by climate change, according to scientists. As the soil and vegetation dry up, they become less able to retain water, so extreme rainstorms trigger floods and erosion (Katwala, Amit. "How Long Droughts Make Flooding Worse." *Wired*, 19 August 2022. www. wired.com/story/drought-causing-floods).

Ecology for Eli

This poem derives from family-history research. Eli George Dodson was the brother of my great-great-grandfather, my uncle four generations removed. The historian Megan Kate Nelson estimates that two million trees were killed during the Civil War, one of the first ecological disasters in U.S. history. General Ulysses S. Grant told Sheridan to "eat out Virginia clear and clear as far as they go, so that crows flying over it for the balance of the season will have to carry their provender with them." A New York surgeon, Daniel M. Holt, wrote of his remembrance of the Battle of Spotsylvania Court House in 1864, "Trees are perfectly riddled with bullets." The word *ecology* can be traced back to 1873, coined by zoologist Ernst Haeckel.

The Healing Landscape

A recent study investigates the significance of landscape therapy, or *the healing landscape* concept. It asserts that the pandemic is a turning point in the reorientation of ecology towards understanding how nature preservation can sustain human society and health (Golubchikov, Yuri N. "Healing Through the Landscape." *International Journal of Hydrology*, 5, 4 [2021], 202-204).

Holy Trees

The following are biblical references (KJV): "mulberry trees" from 2 Sam 5:24; "fruitful bough by a well, whose branches run over the wall" from Gen 49:22; "the waters were made sweet" from Exod 15:25; "the oaks of Mamre" from Gen 18:1; and "the palm tree of Deborah" from Judg 4:5.

Birthright

This poem uses several phrases in Gaelic as a nod to my Ulster heritage as I speak about a deeper belonging. The word *dúcas* describes the understanding of land, people, and culture. *Ag fillead ar do dúcas* means returning to one's native place and also the rediscovery of who one is. *Caim* is the word for a Celtic braided circle, a symbol of protection.

Dogwood Ahimsa

Ahimsa is the ancient Indian principle of nonviolence that applies to all living beings.

Faces of the Poorest and the Weakest

The line "the face of the poorest and the weakest" refers to Gandhi's last known piece of writing, "The Talisman."

Medicine Woods and Monkey Wrenches

In the dialect of Southern Appalachia, this poem mentions 'sang, or ginseng.

The Ballad of Biophilia

Biophilia is a word attached to a hypothesis by Edward O. Wilson that suggests that humans tend to seek connections with nature and other forms of life. The phrase "a mother tree" echoes Suzanne Simard's *Finding the Mother Tree*.

Ansel

This tribute to Ansel Adams reworks a sentence from *The Wilderness Act:* "Where the earth and its community of life are untrammeled by man" (Public Law 88-577, 88th Congress, Second Session, 3 September 1964). "Helios" is the name of Adams' woodpaneled Pontiac station wagon.

The Defenders

Land defenders play a crucial role in protecting the earth against destructive practices, yet more defenders than ever before are being threatened, attacked, or killed. On average, four defenders have been killed every week since December 2015 ("Defending Tomorrow." *Global Witness*, 29 July 2020, www.globalwitness.org/en/campaigns/environmental-activists/defending-tomorrow).

Two Fish and Five Loaves

This poem refers to the feeding of the multitude in John 6, Matt 14, and Mark 6. In this story, Jesus enacts distributive justice, food equity, and the egalitarian access to creation's bounty.

Water Keepers

The allusion to Paddan-Aram and Jacob's removal of the stone from the well comes from Gen 29: 1-10. The access to safe and adequate drinking water is a human right denied to billions. In 2017, 2.2 billion people lacked safely managed water (United Nations). Water injustice is also an issue in the United States, where 77 million people get water from systems with Safe Drinking Water Violations (Natural Resources Defense Council). The words "water is life" echo the Lakota water protectors at Standing Rock.

The Ancestors

This poem is anchored in the idea of *ethnocology*, or when people with a land-based culture share how they perceive the ecosystem that they inhabit.

Rebuilders

The reference to Haggai and Zerubbabel is from Hag 2:2-9 (KJV), and a "living stone" is from 1 Pet 2:4 (KJV).